Greater Than a Tourist - Lake George Area New York USA

50 Travel Tips from a Local

Janine Hirschklau

Order Information: To order this title please email lbrenenc@gmail.com or visit GreaterThanATourist.com. A bulk discount can be provided.

Lock Haven, PA

All rights reserved.

ISBN: 9781521902042

>TOURIST

50 TRAVEL TIPS FROM A LOCAL

Janie Hirschklau

BOOK DESCRIPTION

Are you excited about planning your next trip?

Do you want to try something new while traveling?

Would you like some guidance from a local?

If you answered yes to any of these questions, then this book is just for you.

Greater Than a Tourist by Janine Hirschklau offers the inside scope on the Lake George, NY area. Most travel books tell you how to travel like a tourist. Although there's nothing wrong with that, as a part of the Greater than a Tourist series, this book will give you travel tips from someone who lives at your next travel destination.

In these pages you'll discover local advice that will help you throughout your stay. This book will not tell you exact addresses or store hours but instead will give you an excitement and knowledge from a local that you may not find in other smaller print travel books.   Travel like a local. Slow down, stay in one place, and get to know the people and the culture of a place.

By the time you finish this book, you will be eager and prepared to travel to your next destination.

Janie Hirschklau

TABLE OF CONTENTS

18. Watch the Fireworks from Land

19. Watch Fireworks from the Water

20. Kayaking

21. Paddleboarding

22. Wakeboarding, Water Skiing, and Tubing on the Lake

23. Swimming

24. Weathering the Weather

25. Hiking the East Side of the Lake

26. Hiking the West Side of the Lake

27. Hiking Near the North End of the Lake

28. Spend the Day on an Island

29. Camping on Lake George's Islands

30. Camp on Lake George's Shoreline

31. Watch the Sun Rise

32. Watch the Sun Set

33. Walk to a Waterfall

34. Go Find a Geocache

35. Walk/Run/Bike the Local Trails

36. Watch Out for Wildlife

37. Have an Extreme Adventure

38. Mini-Golf Like a Local

39. Stargaze

40. Local History Comes to Life

41. Appreciate Local Theater

42. Take a Sunset Ride on Horseback

43. Get Wild in Some Whitewater

DEDICATION

This book is dedicated to everyone that makes the Lake George area home. And to Andrew, who brought me to the place I was always meant to be.

Janie Hirschklau

ABOUT THE AUTHOR

Janine Hirschklau is a freelance writer who lives in the Lake George, NY area. Janine loves reading, travelling, and any activities that involve the outdoors, nature, and the occasional unexpected adventure.

Janine loves to travel around the country and around the world, but especially to places where there are plenty of animals to try to pet, much to her husband's chagrin.

I'm just a New Jersey beach bum who, at age 28, unexpectedly found herself living in the place she was always meant to be. Of all the places I've travelled to, Lake George is at the top of my list of most beautiful, and I love calling it home. I truly live in an outdoors-person's paradise. The expansiveness, power, beauty, energy, and serenity of the mountains, lakes, and forests call to my soul and I answer them every chance that I get.

Janie Hirschklau

HOW TO USE THIS BOOK

This book was written by someone who has lived in an area for over three months. The author has made the best suggestions based on their own experiences in the area. Please check that these places are still available before traveling to the area. The goal of this book is to help travelers either dream or experience different locations by providing opinions from a local.

Janie Hirschklau

FROM THE PUBLISHER

Traveling can be one of the most important moments in a person's life. The memories that you have of anticipating going somewhere new or getting to travel are some of the best. As a publisher of the Greater Than a Tourist book series, as well as the popular 50 Things to Know book series, we strive to help you learn about new places, spark your imagination, and inspire you.

Thought this book you will find something for every traveler. Wherever you are and whatever you do I wish you safe fun, and inspiring travel.

Lisa Rusczyk Ed. D.
CZYK Publishing

Janie Hirschklau

WELCOME TO > TOURIST

Lake George itself is a massive 32 miles in length. Quite a few towns, villages, and hamlets touch its beautiful shoreline. Though it is impossible to make it a completely comprehensive guide to the area, consider this as just some friendly suggestions based on my experience.

That being the case, much of this book reflects personal opinion. Everyone has different tastes, preferences, and circumstances, but I've tried hard to cover a wide range of these, making it so that there is something for everyone. Not everyone will agree with me and that is ok—I just want everyone to have a safe and happy vacation no matter what they decide to do.

The majority of the information in this book is centered on the Lake George Village area and summer-time activities. This covers the area and time of year when most people tend to visit. I've tried to include other towns, seasons, and nearby locations as well. Please take into consideration that this area is surrounded by an abundance of wildlife and nature. Keep it clean, do your research, and respect the power of the natural world. It is a magnificent thing, but a healthy measure of caution is the wisest course.
I hope you are able to get a glimpse of my home area through a local's eyes, and come to love it as much as I do.

Janie Hirschklau

1. Getting Around

There is good reason why almost all of the locals own a vehicle--public transportation is scarce and walking is often not an option. There are so many great things to see and do in the area, but it can be difficult and expensive to get around without a vehicle. Other than Lake George Village and the main business section of Bolton Landing, which are easily walkable, there are few to no sidewalks. If you want a hair-raising, adrenaline filled adventure, I definitely would not choose the one that includes walking or biking some of the winding main roads outside of those towns. Save the adrenaline rush for something safer, like para-sailing.

The majority of visitors to the area drive here, but if you are flying, taking a bus or a train to the region, I highly recommend that you rent a vehicle for the duration of your visit.

If you do find yourself without a set of wheels, there are a few taxi companies that provide services to the local area, but they are based out of nearby towns. Don't count on Uber because, as of this writing, it does not exist in this area.

There really isn't any local bus service, except from June to Labor Day. During that time buses/trolleys run between Glens Falls and Lake George Village. There's also bus service between Lake George Village, Hearthstone Campground, and Bolton Landing. You can find a schedule at the Greater Glens Falls Transit website.

2. Finding the Best Places to Stay

For me, one of the worst things about travelling to a new area is arriving exhausted, only to find out that your accommodations are not all their internet photos made out them to be. Who wants to start their vacation being disappointed or even worse, grossed out by the room they need to sleep in for the next several days? There are plenty of places to stay in Lake George, and as with anywhere, some rate higher than others on the skeeve-o-meter. While most places are fine (there's even a brand new Adirondack style Courtyard Marriot in the middle of Lake George Village which is very nice), as a local there are a couple of places I would recommend. These are particularly nice and have a little something special about them.

Romeo and Guilietta's Hideaway on West St. in Lake George is an adorable and quiet little bed and breakfast a few blocks off of the main drag. Most rooms are in a newly renovated building in a well-kept little yard behind the main house. The proprietors, who lived in Italy for several years, have beautifully updated the rooms and building to give them a classic Italian feel. This place is especially recommended for couples or groups that want to stay in separate rooms that are close to each other.

For families or groups, The Quarters at Lake George are terrific townhouses right on the lake just north of the main village. My husband and I stayed there for our first wedding anniversary and I loved every bit of it. Multiple bedrooms, huge corner jacuzzi tubs, and fireplaces give the accommodations a special touch and make this place feel like home. Their docks also offer nice views of the lake for any time of day.

Even though it's pretty touristy, I feel like the Great Escape Lodge is worth mentioning. I'm partial to places with the Adirondack lodge look as I find it to be very warm and cozy. Due to having an indoor waterpark, the lodge largely attracts families with kids. However, it does have a small, but relaxing spa. Prices are a bit higher than an independent spa, but if you feel like treating yourself, it's a nice place to do it.

If you have a little extra money in your accommodations budget, I feel like the Sagamore Hotel and resort is also worth mentioning. This place attracts a lot of out-of-towners as well, but for good reason. The resort is on its own island, easily accessible by bridge. The main hotel building is quite impressive. An unusual style for the area, it's the picture of 19th century opulence. One of my favorite things about this place is eating on their fantastic restaurant porch overlooking the lake. That being said, I think that the condos on the resort property are a better all-around deal if you are going to stay. If you want the full local experience, many websites have private cabins and homes to rent. This is a good way to spend time outside of the main tourist areas, and feel like your living like a local. As with these suggested places and others, rooms get booked up pretty quickly, so make sure you plan ahead and give yourself enough time to stay somewhere really great.

3. Go Food Shopping Like a Local

With regard to towns right on the lake, supermarkets are pretty scarce. Lake George Village has a very small supermarket in town that is good for a few basics, but overall, it's in *serious* need of an update. The supermarket in Bolton Landing is slightly better, but basically the same story. If you're at the north end of the lake, there is a Walmart in Ticonderoga where you can get just about anything you might need (and probably lots of stuff you don't need, but you're on vacation!).

If you're willing to go a little bit out of the way, or go food shopping before you reach your destination (especially if you're headed to the north or eastern parts of the lake), there several more options. Just south of Lake George in the town of Queensbury you will find two Super Walmarts, Hannaford, Aldi's , and Price Chopper supermarkets. If you head just north of the Lake George Village, there is a nice new Price Chopper in the town of Warrensburg.

4. Start the Day Off Right with Breakfast (or Brunch)

There are a number of places that serve breakfast in Lake George and Bolton Landing, and some hotels even offer breakfast (though I hardly count a continental breakfast to be anything more than a snack to get me to real breakfast). But seeing as breakfast is the most important meal of the day (or at least the most delicious in some opinions), you're going to want to breakfast like a local. To breakfast like a local means that you will need to leave the immediate area around the lake, but it's worth the very short road trip. If you get off of the Northway at exit 19 and make a right turn, you'll find my two favorite options.

On the right side of the road is the Ambrosia Diner. As a native New Jerseyian, I'm quite fussy when it comes to diners anywhere else, so the fact that it passes my own little snobbish diner test says a lot about it. Ambrosia has pretty much everything you want in a breakfast-good food, fair prices, and quick, friendly service. If you're looking for something a little more country-gourmet, The Silo on the opposite side of the road is my other choice. It's a really cute little barnwood-type place, and like the diner, you'll find good food and decent prices. It gets pretty busy there, and so as you can imagine it's a little slower than the diner. But if you're not in a hurry, it's worth spending some time there for a leisurely breakfast.

5. Get Your Coffee Fix

If you come into the area and expect to find a Starbucks or even a Dunkin' Donuts on every corner, I'm here to warn you now to perish the thought. I'm more of a mid-afternoon coffee drinker myself, but I would hate for anyone to wake up in the morning in a caffeine-deficient haze and not know what to do. Of course, many hotels and motels provide some coffee choices for their guests, but that wouldn't be doing coffee like a local now, would it?

In case you were wondering, there is a Starbucks and Dunkin' Donuts off of exit 19 in nearby Queensbury. However, there are a few local coffee options that are just as good, if not better, and they don't require you to leave the lake area.

My top pick is Café Vero which is located just a few blocks south of the main portion of Lake George village. I'm what you might call a "dessert coffee" type of girl, so I love the fact that they have so many coffee flavor options. I'm also dairy intolerant, so I'm thrilled that I can have a latte with almond or soy milk. As a fun finishing touch, they often do little artistic designs in your coffee foam. Sometimes it's the little things that make a difference. Conveniently located right in the main part of the village is the new Café 185. Like Café Vero, they also have a more specialty-type coffee menu. But it was their customer service was outstanding in my experience. The owners work in the café, and they are very interested in making sure that you're happy and satisfied with what you get (in my opinion if you're going to pay a premium for specialty coffees, you SHOULD get exactly what you want).

They even had me taste my drink before ringing me out, just in case I wanted any changes to be made. Great customer service that goes above and beyond is always a big plus in my book.

Once you're outside of the Lake George Village area, your coffee pickins' get much slimmer. There are a few delis and small markets that have coffee. Bolton Landing has a small coffee shop in town as well. Perhaps somewhat unexpectedly though, a great number of locals prefer the coffee from the Stewart's Shops (there's one in Bolton and one in Ticonderoga). If you want no fuss, make-it-yourself, inexpensive coffee, this is your kind of place.

6. Parking in Town

There are so many great things about Lake George Village, but trying to park during peak season is definitely not one of them. During the summer in particular, you might spend some time looking for a place to park. I'm shocked and overjoyed whenever we find a spot on the main strip because it's like hitting the jackpot—very exciting, but not too unlikely. We usually go straight to the further side-streets to park, especially the streets closer to the ends of town.

Your chances of finding parking right away are much greater here, though it does mean having to do a little walking (some exercise is good for the body though, no?). One very important point to remember is--and I cannot stress this enough--bring enough quarters for the parking meters. One quarter only gets you 15 min of parking, so plan accordingly. Even as a local, I constantly forget to bring enough quarters with us, and we have not been immune to the long arm of the village parking police, who are very diligent about handing out parking violations.

7. Eating Your Way Through Lake George-- Restaurants on the Lake

From Lake George village to Bolton Landing, you have quite a number of restaurants right on the lake. These are quite tempting due to their having such beautiful views, but as locals we are generally not tempted to these eateries. For the most part, we find them to be crowded, expensive, and serving mediocre food (a few are even less than mediocre).

One of the few exceptions to this are the two main restaurants in the Sagamore Hotel in Bolton. La Bella Vita is a more upscale Italian restaurant. Although it is not necessarily formal, keep in mind that the unofficial dress code for this restaurant is nicer than casual. Their food is great, the service is top notch, and they have a pretty nice wine selection. It's definitely one of the nicest places to celebrate an anniversary or special occasion, something we've done many times. The best part, though, is eating outside on their gorgeous porch area which overlooks the lake (or near the windows inside if it's cold outside). It's just so beautiful out there and for me it makes this place the whole package.

Janie Hirschklau

The second option I'd choose is a nice casual restaurant downstairs called Mr. Brown's Pub. They also have seating outside in nicer weather. The inside is very nice as well, being done in Adirondack lodge style with plenty of log features. The pub style food is good here, too--they make an amazing French onion soup.

Unfortunately, there really aren't good views of the lake from this location. However, on a nice evening we grab a drink after dinner and walk down to the water to sit in the chaise lounges and just soak in the scenery. Although these can also get a little crowded, it's worth the wait, making a reservation, or going at a less busy time.

8. Eating Your Way Through Lake George--Off the Beaten Path

Sometimes the roads less travelled contain the best restaurants. There are three that we particularly love for their food and atmosphere.

The first is The View restaurant at Dunham's Bay Resort. I feel is seriously place is seriously underrated. Their delicious food comes with an equally delicious view. Even though it's not directly on the lake, it is right across from the water. If you can get one of the few seats by the window, you will have a fantastic view of the lake and its particularly lovely at sunset. It's a nice, quiet, out of the way place to have a pleasant meal--no fighting the crowds necessary. Second is Le Roux, a French bistro a little farther from Dunham's Bay. The food here is exceptional. Since it is done in the French style, don't expect large portions. Their food is so rich and wonderful though, that portion size is not an issue for us. For dessert, try their flourless chocolate cake, which is pretty much a slice of fudgy heaven. It does get busy here, so it's best to make a reservation.

Janie Hirschklau

The third restaurant we frequently eat at is The Log Jam. If you want a restaurant that feels like the Adirondacks, this place is about as lodge-like as it gets. Basically a big log cabin, it exudes warm and atmosphere. During the colder months, you can eat right in front of a number of working wood fireplaces. Even when it's busy, you can often grab a table in the seat-yourself area near the bar, and you will still be served there. I'm particularly fond of their salad bar, and I often go specifically for that.

9. Eating Your Way Through Lake George--Ice Cream and Other Sweets

It would be crazy to talk about eating locally without talking about desserts—it's the best part! Some of the best desserts are in the least obvious places. For example, you'll actually find some pretty great gelato and sorbet inside the Lake George Olive Oil Company on the main Street in Lake George.

This may be surprising, but one of the best places for ice cream is at the Stewart's Shops (attached to the gas stations). Stewart's has their own brand of ice cream, and they come in a host of flavors. You can buy gallons to take away, but they also have an ice cream bar right in the shops. Here you can get sundaes, cones, and cups with a variety of toppings.

Many locals also love Martha's ice cream which is located across from the Great Escape amusement park. We personally don't think there is anything special about their ice cream, but most people love it and it is almost insanely crowded for most of the time that they are open.

If you're looking for baked treats, Lake George Baking Company is the only actual bakery in Lake George or Bolton. Located on a side street in the village, it's not in the most obvious location. My husband absolutely loves their Italian pastries in particular, and I'm very happy that they now have a few gluten free options.

10. Seek out and Taste the Local Honey

Growing up, I never liked honey. I never realized that this was due to the fact that I had never tried fresh, local honey. Once I moved into the area, I tried it in order to help with seasonal allergies, and I was hooked. The taste, consistency, and freshness were a world of difference from any commercial honey that I had previously tried. Many places that sell local honey also sell raw honey (which tastes quite different but has tons of health benefits), and honey with the comb. You may be able to find some in Lake George and Bolton if you look around their Adirondack type shops, but you may have to travel a little to find some. The Warrensburg Farmers Market just north of the village carries local honey as well as Pure N' Simple in Glens Falls. Try localharvest.org to find a list of other locations.

11. Try Gourmet Olive Oils and Balsamic Vinegars

Right in the thick of Lake George Village, you will find some very fine gourmet food items. The Lake George Olive Oil Company has a store right on the main street across from Shepard's Park. Although the olive oils are not locally made, they are high quality and definitely worth a sample. In fact, you can go into the store and sample any one of their oils or balsamic vinegars. They have quite a large variety of different flavor infused olive oils and balsamic vinegars, some of which I never would have thought could work. Tuscan herb, Dill, and Butter infused olive oils are among my favorites.

Fruit infused balsamic flavors making surprisingly wonderful additions to desserts. I must warn though, that as with all premium quality foods, you are going to pay a higher price. They do sell small bottles, so if you would like to buy more than one flavor, this is a more affordable option. This is especially so for oils you might not use every day.

12. Taste the Local Wines

Though the Adirondack Winery uses grapes from across New York State, their wines are locally made right in Queensbury. It's fairly inexpensive to do a tasting, and it's a nice way to spend an hour. I might be in the minority, but I like my wine with some easily detectable fruit flavor. Adirondack Winery has some delightful fruit wines (pineapple, mango, sangria to name a few) that are crisp and not overly sweet.

Their prices are affordable as well, averaging $14-16 per bottle. If you're feeling like you could go for a sugar fix in the form of an adult beverage, their Lake George store serves refreshing wine slushies.

13. Shopping the Outlets

The Lake George outlets contain some big brand stores that aren't available anywhere else in the area. I do shop at some of these stores in the off season, but during the summer months we tend to avoid this area as much as possible. Especially on rainy days, you will find a great deal of car and pedestrian traffic on the one road passing through the outlets, making it sometimes difficult and time-consuming to get around.

Many people think of outlets as big name brands at discount prices, and this can be true at times. Overall, I don't usually find these outlets to be much of a bargain, nor heavily discounted. It is good to be aware that some outlets offering discounted prices also sell inferior products made specifically for their outlet stores. I'm not saying that you shouldn't shop here, but do your research and let the buyer beware.

There is one locally owned store near the north end of the outlets that stands out. The Sox Market is my favorite outlet store for a number of reasons, and I mainly love it for their super fun and funky socks. Some of my softest and best loved socks have come from this store. Here I've also gotten many person-specific novelty socks to give as fun gifts. If you're looking to shop for something fun and a little different, this is the place.

Janie Hirschklau

Lake George is without comparison, the most beautiful water I ever saw; formed by a contour of mountains into a basin... finely interspersed with islands, its water limpid as crystal, and the mountain sides covered with rich groves... down to the water-edge: here and there precipices of rock to checker the scene and save it from monotony."

-- Thomas Jefferson, May 31, 1791

Janie Hirschklau

14. See the Lake From the Water--Boat Tours

Since Lake George is 32 miles long, it's impossible to really see it's full loveliness from any one spot on land. Since most visitors to the area do not have a boat, I would hate for so many people to miss out on its immense and impressive beauty. That is why, even though it's a touristy thing to do, I recommend taking one of the boat tours out of Lake George village. A couple of the boat companies offer tours specifically for sightseeing on the lake. These tours are usually not very long--one or two hours--and are fairly inexpensive. Although the tour boats don't go up and down the entire length of the lake, it does give a very nice vantage point for seeing some of it's gorgeous features. Most tour boats have a concession stand and bar which are open for the duration of the trip. My suggestion is to grab a drink and go get a seat near the railing of the completely open top deck. Then there's nothing left to do but sit back, relax, and enjoy the scenery (in that order).

15. See Lake George From Above--Prospect Mountain

If you aren't hiker, you don't need to miss a great view from the top of a mountain. Prospect Mountain has a paved road with various lookouts on the way to the top. Once you are at the topmost parking lot--which does not go to the very top--you have 2 options for reaching the peak. There is a shuttle bus that comes by every few minutes, allowing you to hop on for a ride at no additional cost. If you're feeling energetic and want to stretch your legs, there is a short, but somewhat steep, trail to the top (don't let the word "steep" scare you too much--I see children and older people walking it all the time). From the peak, you will be able to see the southern end of the lake along with surrounding towns. On a clear day can even see the mountains of Vermont. There isn't a whole lot to do at the top, but if you would like, you are able to picnic there. Overall a nice view if you're OK with spending a few dollars for it.

I would like to mention that there is a well-traveled trail that can be hiked from the bottom to the top. If you want to do a great hike though, save your energy and see my tips for more worthwhile hikes.

16. Boating Like a Local--Where to Launch and When

There are very few public boat launches on Lake George. The most popular and well-trafficked of these is at Million Dollar Beach on the southern end of the lake. Here you will have to pay a fee to park and launch your boat. Even though it's a very nice, easy place to launch, it's extremely popular during the summer and parking for boat trailers is limited. You may get there and find that there are no spaces left to park your boat trailer (there are no places to park it in town, either). We usually call ahead to the beach or Lake George information center to find out if there are any open spaces, just to get an idea if it's worth the trip (they cannot hold a space, and even if there are spaces open when you call, it's no guarantee there will be still be open spaces when you arrive). If we find out that the lot is full, we usually wait until after 3pm to launch, there being a better chance of finding a spot at that time of day.

There are also public launches in the town of Hague and even farther north at Rogers Rock Campground. A word of warning about that--you will have to tow your boat up and over a winding mountain road to reach those launches. This can be somewhat difficult and take upwards of and hour from the village area. Some private marinas allow public boats to launch, but they can charge an exorbitant fee ($40-$50) to do so. You'll also need to be back at the marina to take out before they close (usually 7-8pm). Some marinas are closed on holidays, weekends, or Sundays, so you need to check and plan ahead.

There is a marina around Dunham's Bay that offers launch from a creek area just south of the bay, but to get into the lake you have to navigate your boat under a bridge with very low clearance. In order to make this, your boat cannot sit more than 4 feet or so off the water. Check your boat measurements (including your windshield height) and double check clearance with the marina (water levels can vary) before you attempt to launch here.

17. Boating Like a Local--Where to Hang Out on the Lake

While boating up and down the lake is a very nice way to view the gorgeous scenery, you might want to drop anchor and relax somewhere. There are many places to hang out, but you cannot (and definitely should not) do this just anywhere. There are two bays on the east side of the lake that are great for throwing out your anchor, relaxing, and swimming. Closer to the southern end of the lake and around Assembly Point, (across from Long Island) there are three bays. The middle bay, Sandy Bay, offers anchored buoys to which you can tie off your boat. This area has water levels ranging from fairly shallow to very shallow towards the back end. Its shallow water makes it a great place to cool off, swim, or just float, especially for kids. When in the water, please be mindful that there can be a bit of boat traffic as boats come into and leave the area. Farther north, across from the town of Bolton, is Log Bay. This is also a shallow area, but there are no buoys for tying off a boat. You will need a good anchor for this location as the bottom is mostly sand and there is a tendency for boats to drift. This area is known to be somewhat of a party location. Music, boisterous boaters, and drinking are common here. If you love a party atmosphere, this is the spot for you. If you have children, you might want to think twice about anchoring here, or at least wait until later in the day to park.

18. Watch the Fireworks from Land

Several of the towns on the lake put on a fireworks display during holidays or holiday weekends. The village of Lake George not only sets off an impressive fireworks display at these times, they do so all summer long on. You can see them for free every Thursday night during the summer and on weekends with special events.

Lake George village consistently does some of the best fireworks displays I've ever witnessed, and it's definitely worth going to see. For that reason, there are massive crowds gathered around the lake to watch. Being so, you can imagine how slow and difficult it can be to get to your car and leave town after the show. My husband and I learned our lesson one night after it took us an hour to get out of the village. So here is how we watch fireworks as locals.

Park near the farthest edges of town for a quick escape. If you park near the hill at southern end of town, you can actually view the fireworks right from the street. We have done this and were able to run right to our car afterwards, quickly beating the crowd out of town. Another option is to park near or in the Million Dollar Beach lot (you'll have to check with the rangers first to see what time they will close the lot gate. Don't get locked in!). From this area, you have a great view of the fireworks over the lake. When it's time to leave, use GPS to take one of the side roads back to where you are going.

19. Watch Fireworks from the Water

Whether you have a boat or not, watching the fireworks from the water makes an awesome event even more amazing. There's nothing like sitting under the wide-open night sky as colors burst and rain down around you.

If you don't have a boat, several of the large boat companies offer fairly inexpensive fireworks cruises (they are usually only an hour or so). You can grab a drink and sit on the open top deck. This is an excellent way to watch the show.

If you do have your own boat and you launched out of Million Dollar Beach, you may be able to stay out on the lake to view the fireworks from almost directly underneath them. The parking lot gate usually stays open later on nights with fireworks, but to be sure, check with the rangers beforehand (you don't want to be locked in for the night).

Due to the fact that the lake has mountains on either side of it, the boom of the fireworks loudly echoes back and forth over the lake in a series of audial volleys. This creates quite an impressive and unique effect (think French and Indian War type cannon fire). It has also scared the pants off of more than one young child, so if you have any with you, be prepared for that possibility.

20. Kayaking

The waters of Lake George can be quite rough when there is wind and/or a good amount of power boat traffic. This is why I recoil in horror every time I see some poor soul trying to kayak in the middle of the lake or in a location that does not offer some protection from the waves. Don't get me wrong, kayaking is an excellent and beloved activity, but not in open waters or areas with regular boat traffic. This is something we would never do, and I cannot stress enough how dangerous this can be, even for experienced kayakers.

If you really want to kayak on the lake, and I understand why you would, I have a few recommendations. First, go early in the day. Watch the sun come over the mountains, listen for loons, and enjoy the peace. The second is the Northwest Bay boat launch (car top boats only). This launch starts in a small estuary that eventually takes you out into the calmer north section of Northwest Bay. It's a gorgeous paddle through and through, with many different bird species to watch for.

Another great place to paddle is from the boat launch in Roger's Rock State Campground. Though there is boat traffic in this area, if you hug the coast it's generally not too rough of a ride. You can kayak right under the fabled Rogers Rock, an immense cliff that comes climbs straight out of the water. If you want nice easy flat water, Trout Lake in Bolton Landing is your best bet.

21. Paddleboarding

My advice about paddleboarding is very similar to the advice that I give to kayakers, only more emphatic. Paddleboard early morning or late day. Once there is boat traffic on the lake, this activity can be difficult. Even if you have paddleboarded in an ocean setting, there is still a factor of danger with boats buzzing by at high speeds. Though it is the primary responsibility of the boat operator, you cannot depend on them to see you in the water, especially in an open area.

The Rogers Rock area and the northern end of Northwest Bay offer some sanctuary for paddleboarders. Right outside the swimming area of Veteran's Memorial Park beach in Bolton Landing does as well.

If you would like some flat water to paddleboard on, Trout Lake in Bolton is a nice area. If you are closer to the southern end of the lake, there are a number of slow, flatwater sections of the Hudson River in Queensbury and Lake Luzerne that can be paddled. Lake Luzerne itself is also a beautiful place to paddleboard (it's also one of my favorite places for a relaxing kayak) and you will not find any boats over 10 horsepower on that small lake.

22. Wakeboarding, Water Skiing, and Tubing on the Lake

I have many times been terrified on behalf of those that I see (especially children) doing any of the above-mentioned activities in the middle of the lake. Those doing these activities tend to fall into the water rather quickly, leaving little time for boat traffic to see or avoid them. I'm not saying that these types of accidents happen often-but I'm sure I speak for everyone when I say no one wants it to ever happen.

During the summer months, the waters in the middle of the lake can be quite choppy or rough, especially for wakeboarders and water skiers. So, at the risk of sounding like a broken record, my advice is going to be similar to what I've mentioned to kayakers and paddleboarders. The best time to water-ski or wakeboard is early morning or early evening. I personally don't think I've ever wakeboarded on Lake George until after 5-6pm. The waters start to calm and the boat traffic starts to lighten after this time. In the summer, you'll still have at least a couple hours of sunlight left. Another safer option for these activiies is to do them in any of the large bays on the lake. On a map you can find Dunham's Bay, Harris Bay, Warner Bay, and Northwest Bay to name of few. These are the spots that the majority of locals go to when they want to let out their ropes and ride.

Janie Hirschklau

"It's a place people go to escape, A place made of pine trees, cabins, and lakes, But no matter how far you drive, There's no sign to say "You've arrived", So just follow your heart till you find...Your special place that brings piece of mind, As you breathe in the air and unwind... Your cares are all left behind, It's no mystery where the northwoods start, When you arrive up north, You'll know in your heart."

-Susan Kindler

Janie Hirschklau

23. Swimming

Lake George's amazing crystal waters are hard to resist, and I find that I cannot be near it without being incredibly tempted to jump and take a swim. Most visitors go to Million Dollar Beach located in the Village of Lake George. They have a concession stand, bathroom, and showers, and if that's what you want, it's a beach with a gorgeous view looking north. However, as locals, we almost never swim here or in nearby Shepard's Park for a variety of reasons. Mainly, these beaches and waters tend to be dirtier due to higher volumes of people. I find that there are much nicer (and sometimes less crowded) places to swim.

Veteran's Memorial Park Beach in Bolton is an excellent place to swim and its scenery is quite lovely. They do have a nice bathhouse there, and a grassy area for picnics as well. My other preferred swimming spot is at the beach in Roger's Rock State Campground. As it is a state park, you can pay a small fee to enjoy the beach and boat launch for a day. The swimming area isn't massive, but it's big enough and generally not super crowded. From this location, you'll have some of the most beautiful views you will find from a public beach area.

24. Weathering the Weather

The weather in this area can be quite temperamental, and even somewhat unpredictable, any time of the year. Due to its varying topography and land elevations, what is happening weather-wise in one spot is not necessarily what is happening even a very short distance away. Likewise, what is happening down at lake level is not necessarily the same at higher elevations. This is very important information to keep in mind if you are camping, hiking, or doing any outdoor activity where you will be exposed to the elements for a length of time.

In the summer, strong thunderstorms with high winds (sometimes at hurricane force speeds), downpours, and hail can whip across the lake with surprising intensity. In cooler months, you can have perfectly lovely weather on the ground, but by the time you've hiked to the top of a mountain, you might wonder whether you've actually entered a completely different climate zone (and you kind of did). Conditions can include fog, rain, snow and other frozen precipitation, wind, or any combination of these.

I included this section because, even as a local, I've been caught unprepared and unaware in more than one situation. So keep an eye on weather predictions, don't underestimate Mother Nature, prepare thoroughly, dress appropriately for the season, go outside and have fun.

25. Hiking the East Side of the Lake

There are so many great hikes here that you can spend a lifetime exploring and never get bored. For that reason, I've broken up my hiking tips into sections with the best hike or two in each area. If you're up for a moderate hike with some tougher spots, Black Mountain is worth the climb. There are two different routes to the top--one being easier than the other--but I recommend doing the whole 7.7 mile loop if you can. Being the highest peak in the Lake George area, the top offers some of the nicest and farthest views, especially from the fire tower located there.

If you have less time and/or energy, nearby Shelving Rock is a good option. A series of switchbacks that climb fairly gently over a mile or so, it doesn't take much time or effort to reach the top. During the colder months, there is a nice view looking towards the south end of the lake. Tree foliage in warmer months obscures part of this view, but it's made up for by the divinely delicious wild blueberries that grow at the top.

26. Hiking the West Side of the Lake

My top hiking picks for this area are both in Bolton Landing, with both trailheads not being far from each other (not close enough to walk though). The Pinnacle is probably the best view for the least amount of effort. A little over a mile of rocky switchbacks brings you up to a ledge (with a bench!) overlooking the lake near the Sagamore Hotel. The view is breathtaking and unobscured. It is not set back far from the lake, making it easy to clearly see boats and small nearby islands. Just a word of caution, be very careful near the edge of the ledge as it is a long, steep drop-off.

Nearby Thomas Mountain is also a great hike with a fun surprise at the top. A relatively short but rocky hike brings you to an opening at the peak. Although the view is nice, this mountain is set farther back from the lake, so your view is not as detailed or expansive. There is however, a nice view of the surrounding mountains. The best part of this peak though, is the log cabin at the top. It is empty except for a log sofa bench, but anyone who wants to claim it for the night is free to sleep in its upper loft or main living area. It also has a porch and an "unofficial" fire pit out front.

27. Hiking Near the North End of the Lake

My favorite hike in this area is to the top of Roger's Rock. Located within the campground, the trailhead is difficult to find. It is unmarked and located between two campsites (ask for directions at the check-in booth). Although it is pretty short in distance, this hike is incredibly fun, but not for the faint-hearted. Very steep sections require rock scramble-type climbing (I've even had to use tree roots and branches to pull myself up), and tiny narrow ledges require some care and agility. I personally love this kind of challenge, and the view from the top is an added bonus. It is one of the best views that you can climb to, and it's particularly beautiful towards the end of the day. Use extreme caution at the top as there is nothing to prevent disastrous falls.

Janie Hirschklau

28. Spend the Day on an Island

Well it may not be a tropical island, but the islands on Lake George have their own beauty and appeal. You can swim, picnic, and relax on one of the day use sites designated on a number of islands. These sites are only accessible by boat and you'll need to get a day pass at a ranger's station on either Glen Island or Narrow Island (Norowal Marina in Bolton may still have a ranger's station so you can call and check). The sites cannot be reserved and are first come first serve, so you need to get there early in order to get a site during busy times.

Sarah Island and Hazel Island near Paradise Bay are my picks for the best islands hang out on. These are a bit more private and quiet and make nice spots for swimming. These islands also have beautiful views, grills, and areas to make a campfire.
If you can't get a site on either of these islands, and you optimally want the most sun and good swimming, check a map at the ranger's station for islands on the east side of the lake, and look for sites that face away from the middle of the lake. I wanted to mention that if you picnic on Speaker Heck Island, there is a bald eagle's nest high in one of the trees on the west side of the island. Although it's a protected site, there is nothing illegal or preventing you from getting near the tree and trying to get a peck at this impressive bird.

29. Camping on Lake George's Islands

If you love camping and have access to a powerboat, I highly recommend camping on one of the islands. Stunning sunsets, spacious campsites, the sound of whippoorwills and gently lapping water lulling you to sleep at night-it's hard to get more magical than that.

If you are going to reserve one of the campsites, there are three island groups that you can look under. The Narrow Island group is the farthest north, but it's where we consider the best sites to be located. It is a beautiful area and it's somewhat removed from the heavier boat traffic near the southern part of the lake (although boat traffic can be heavy at the mouth of the Narrows and Northwest Bay). Any way you slice it though, the islands and surrounding lake will be busy in the summer months, making mid-September a good option for avoiding the heavier crowds. The weather is often still warm during the day, as is the lake temperature. Nights are a little cooler, but it's nothing a campfire and sleeping bag can't fix. You're also less likely to experience the severe storms that I mentioned earlier. No matter when you go, don't forget to pack the toilet paper-the only bathroom facilities on most islands are little wooden outhouses that provide you with a rustic experience.

30. Camp on Lake George's Shoreline

There are a number of campgrounds on or near the lake. Some are private and some are state campgrounds. If you can do without electrical hook-ups, one of the state campgrounds is an inexpensive way to camp.

In case you hadn't guessed from some of my previous tips, I'm very partial to Roger's Rock State Campground. It's a large campground, so it's fairly easy to get a site any time of year (sometimes even last minute). The loop that includes sites 196-244 is probably the most private and out-of-the-way, and the trailhead to Roger's Rock is in this area. The beach here is gorgeous, and it's a favorite place to swim and kayak.

It doesn't get as busy here as on the islands, but if you want a quieter time, mid-September usually has warmer days and cooler nights for camping perfection.

Janie Hirschklau

"A lake carries you into recesses of feeling otherwise impenetrable."

-William Wordsworth

Janie Hirschklau

31. Watch the Sun Rise

The sun rising over the ocean is a spectacular sight, but there is something about watching the sun come up over a mountain range that appears quite heavenly. You would think that having a high vantage point to see this would be the best thing, but watching from lake level gives you a whole different show. From a lower vantage point, you can watch with anticipation as the sky slowly brightens and the sun starts to shyly peek over the mountain tops before bursting out in its full glory.

Sitting on a boat along the western shore is the most obvious way to get a great view of the sunrise, but if that isn't possible for one reason or another, there are other options for optimal viewing. The public docks in Huddle Bay are probably going to be the most private spot. It's bring-your-own-chair, but the lake will provide the peaceful beauty. You will also have a nice view from the docks in Roger's Park in Bolton Landing. If you are closer to the southern end of the lake and can't muster up to make it north, the docks at Shepard's Park over in Lake George village offer a fairly lengthy view of the east side of the lake.

32. Watch the Sun Set

It goes without saying that you will need to be on the eastern side of the lake for this, but it's a little easier said than done. Unlike watching the sunrise, there are not a whole lot of places to just stop and watch the sunset on this side of the lake. But that's not to say there aren't any.

Hulett's Park is a perfect area to eat a picnic dinner and watch the sun set after a day of swimming or kayaking at its beach. If you are up for a mini-adventure, the gazebo at the top of the Pilot Knob Preserve offers a spectacular view of the sunset from a higher vantage point.

Of course if you have a boat, you can watch the sun set from just about anywhere along the eastern shore. Shelving Rock Bay and Log Bay are particularly nice open areas to see the sun slowly slip behind the mountains and paint the sky an array of colors. If you are not staying on the lake, just be mindful of the time and how long it will take you to get back to where you launched.

33. Walk to a Waterfall

The hiking areas around the lake do not provide prolific opportunities to see waterfalls, but there are falls to be seen. A very easy hike/walk will bring you to Shelving Rock Falls. The falls are very rocky and have a lot of interesting details to look at, but it is also a slippery area, so use caution. From the road, it is a very short distance to the falls, so it might be worth your while to combine this with another hike in the area, or continue down the trail to walk along the lake.

If you hike up the Pilot Knob Preserve trail and continue past the gazebo at the top (after first pausing to take in the scenery from the gazebo, of course), another 20-25 minutes you will bring you to a lovely little waterfall. The waterfall itself is not impressively huge, but it's a nice slice of nature that makes the whole trail a perfect little package.

34. Go Find a Geocache

Geocaching is like a fun little treasure hunt that can be done with a geocaching app on a smart phone or with instructions printed out ahead of time. Some geocachers leave clues, riddles, or outright instructions on where to find the cache. Once found, you can leave your name and/or take a little trinket from the box depending on the type of cache. If you do take something, be prepared to leave something in return for the next treasure hunters.

This is a particularly fun activity in on the heavily wooded trails on the east side of Lake George. There are many terrific hiding spots here, making it an enjoyable challenge. Most trails have one or more geocaches, so it's an entertaining side activity for your hike. Or, map out your caches on several trails and locations for an all day, multi-location treasure hunt.

35. Walk/Run/Bike the Local Trails

The Warren County bike trail is a paved trail that runs 12 miles from Glens Falls right down to Lake George near Million Dollar Beach. It is a pleasant and safe way to bike, rollerblade, or walk without being on the road, and it even passes by some historical sites. It is, however, quite hilly. Depending on which way you are going, it can be a quite an uphill climb, so just keep that in mind with regard to fitness and skill level.

Even though walkers are allowed on this trail, a much nicer trail to walk is Rush Pond, just south of the outlets. The trail starts out along the road, but in short distance becomes a dirt path that goes off into the woods. You'll pass over a little wooden bridge, streams, and walk by Rush Pond itself. At a little over 2 miles in length, it's a nice little nature walk.

Even though the region is generally safe, the trails sometimes run through heavily wooded areas, making it wise to always go with a friend.

Janie Hirschklau

36. Watch Out for Wildlife

When you're surrounded by nature, you can expect to come in contact with--well, nature. Deer, bear, foxes, and rattlesnakes are just a few of the animals that live in the area. More elusive animals like loons and even mountain lions can be found near the lake. Most of these animals don't want anything to do with humans, and if everyone just leaves each other alone, all can go on their merry way. But there are precautions that should be kept in mind, especially in wilderness areas.

The black bears that inhabit the area are generally scared of people, especially large groups making a lot of noise. You never want to catch a bear by surprise, so occasionally calling out to let them know you're there will help them to keep their distance. As adorable as bear cubs might be, if you come across any, leave the area immediately.

There will inevitably be an angry mother bear in the vicinity, and you don't want to cross her path. If you are camping, bears, raccoons and other animals are likely to visit during the night to see what you have to eat. Keep food in animal-proof containers or in your vehicle overnight. Some animals are very clever and have learned to open certain containers like coolers, so make sure that everything is secure before going to bed.

Although they really aren't considered animals, it's worth noting that there are 2-3 weeks in May that locals call "black fly" season. These pesty flies are prolific during this period, more so than any other time. They have voracious appetites and will bite, even drawing blood. If you are going out into the woods during this time, be prepared for this situation.

37. Have an Extreme Adventure

Even though the area does provide some sport for adrenaline junkies, this extreme adventure is slightly different. Adirondack Extreme in Bolton Landing is made up of 5 tree top courses comprised of climbing nets, ropes hopping between log swings, moving bridges, and other balance-challenging obstacles. Several ziplines are thrown in to give you an exciting little break from climbing. Of course, you are tethered to safety lines at all times, but it doesn't stop this from being incredibly fun and challenging. Like most activities in the area, it can get crowded during the summer. Consider going early or later season (after mid-September), or book first thing in the morning. Any of those times will generally have less crowds and more comfortable temperatures for this type of physical activity.

Do note that although this activity is slated for a variety of ages and abilities, some level of physical fitness, balance, and agility are going to make this a far more enjoyable experience.

38. Mini-Golf Like a Local

There are a surprising number of mini-golf courses within a small area just south of Lake George village. Some can be on the more expensive side, especially for a family. There are a couple of go-to courses that we like, especially during the summer.
Lumberjack Pass, which is right near the outlets, is a fun course on a hill away from the main fray. It's inexpensive and slated to be the largest mini-golf course in the area. I also find that it is generally less crowded than other courses closer to the village.

Adirondack Golf in Lake Luzerne is also a favorite. We usually find it to be uncrowded right after dinner time. The course is fun and challenging enough for most ages. It's also one of the most inexpensive places to mini-golf. As a bonus, it is attached to the locally-loved Bon's Ice Cream. If you ask me, mini-golf and snacks are a great way to end a day.

39. Stargaze

Nothing gives you perspective or makes you feel so small as gazing out into the expanse of the universe. Lake George has plenty of expanse to gaze into. If you are fortunate enough to be out on the lake late at night--especially in a boat--enormous constellations, multitudes of stars, and the gauzy gases of the Milky Way provide an awe-inspiring backdrop to the looming mountain silhouettes.

If you are stuck on land, Top of the World Golf course in Lake George is a drivable location high up on a hill overlooking the lake. From here you can't see much of the lake at night, but you can look up to catch a sea of stars.

The farther you get from towns and light pollution, the more sky you will be able to see. That's why your best views will be towards the northern end of the lake. Roger's Rock Campground is located away from the fray and their boat docks are a prime place to peep a plethora of stars.

You should also note that during mid-summer, the best time to stargaze is after 10:30pm, well past sunset, giving the sky time to darken.

40. Local History Comes to Life

The Lake George area is rich with colonial and pre-colonial history. It's often celebrated with informative signs in key locations and even occasional reenactments and camps with actors in full dress. If you happen to be in the area during one of the encampment or reenactment weekends, it's very interesting to speak with reenactors, see their tools, tents, clothing, and other accessories of the time period.

Fort William Henry in Lake George village gives you a small piece of history, but it's not the original fort, nor is it in its original location. However, Fort Ticonderoga at the north end of Lake George is still standing in its original location and is a far more impressive structure. It's easy to hear a a guide's stories about the fort and imagine them happening right in front of you. It is a bit of a haul from the south end of the lake, but well worth it for history lovers.

Janie Hirschklau

*"The lake and the mountains have
become my landscape, my real world."*

--Georges Simenon

Janie Hirschklau

41. Appreciate Local Theater

There are a few small local theaters in the area, some of which are open year-round. They have a wide variety of shows for all age ranges, but if you are in the area mid-summer, the Last of the Mohicans outdoor drama at Wild West Ranch is a must-see in my opinion. The troupe does an outstanding job of adapting the novel to the stage.

The story itself is fictional, but its background is based on actual historical events surrounding the surrender of Fort William Henry, and the subsequent massacre of those fleeing the fort. One of the coolest things about this play is that many of the historical events depicted in the book/play happened right where the audience is sitting. It's a masterful piece of living art and history.

42. Take a Sunset Ride on Horseback

Even though there are a variety of stables in the area that offer horseback riding, there's one tour that is really outstanding. Bennett's Stables in Lake Luzerne offers sunset dinner horseback rides to the top of local Beech Mountain.

The ride itself is slow, but you'll steadily wind through beautiful forests as you climb to the top of the mountain. The views from the top are pretty incredible during any time of day, but throw in dinner and a sunset and it's the recipe for one terrific adventure.

43. Get Wild in Some Whitewater

When you want a break from all that flatwater, whitewater rafting is just the adventure to add some excitement to your stay. There are 2 rivers within easy driving distance of the immediate Lake George area that offer whitewater opportunities.

The smaller of the two, the Sacandaga River, is in nearby Lake Luzerne and offers class II & III rapids. You'll spend a refreshing hour paddling the rapids and swimming the flatwater section. It's a good river for families with young children--or if you just feel like getting splashed with a few whitewater waves. Definitely a fun little ride.

The Hudson River gorge which is northwest of Lake George Village is an all-day whitewater trip that includes class III & IV rapids. Due to its somewhat more intense nature, there is an age limit for Hudson River rafting trips. Summer raft trips here are definitely a nice adventure, but the river generally calms down a little bit by this time. If you are the more intrepid sort, and you want the biggest, fastest, wildest whitewater possible, early spring is your time to go (I definitely prefer this time). The spring melt sends higher waters rushing down the river, creating waves that are truly thrilling. Sure, it will be cold outside during that time, but outfitters provide guests with wetsuits and enough adrenaline to keep you warm.

Janie Hirschklau

What most visitors want to know is, "Which whitewater company do I go with?" As a former whitewater guide on both rivers, I've worked for, and with, a number of companies. Some river guides have a reputation for unsafe behavior and less than stellar professionalism. I've seen enough to know who I would want to send my family and friends rafting with. Here is my unbiased advice.

If you are rafting the Sacandaga River, Sacandaga Outdoor Center (SOC) is the outfitter to visit. They are professional and their operation is tip top. They've really worked hard to have a nice clean shop, equipment, and buses for their guests. The guides are also well trained, which is important when your safety is involved. For Hudson River whitewater, Wild Waters has a great operation. Conveniently, their shop is the closest to the Lake George village area. Their guides are also very professional, and while they want to give their guest a fun time, they keep safety high in mind. Their base of operations is very nice, providing indoor bathrooms and showers for guests. They take good care of their equipment, which is not always the case with every outfitter. They also do a nice post-trip dinner for guests.

44. Peep Some Leaves

Fall is a beautiful time in the Lake George area. The weather can still be somewhat warm and pleasant during this time. The leaves start their annual transformation around late September, usually peaking by mid-October. It's a beautiful sight to see the mountains around Lake George carpeted in a vibrant array of colors. Boat traffic has usually died down somewhat, so if you are able to, boat instead of drive for your leaf peeping tour.

Since the weather is cooler than in the summer, it's a great time of year to hike. For leaf viewing over a wide area, I recommend hiking Sleeping Beauty Mountain. It's a moderate hike and from the peak, you can see plenty of colorful leaves near and far. On a clear day, you can even see as far as Gore Mountain, which on occasion can be capped with snow by this time.

If you aren't a hiker, an easy place to get a nice view of the autumn mountains is Roger's Memorial in Bolton Landing. You can have a beautiful backdrop for a picnic, or go stand out on the docks and take it all in.

45. Snowtube and Sled Like a Local

Sure there are commercial snowtubing parks in the area, but my fondest winter memories involved sledding and snowtubing in local parks. Gurney Lane Recreation area, just south of the outlets, is one such place to make those kinds of memories. There's nothing fancy about it-- just a nice, quiet hill in an out of the way park. When the park is open, there is a little hut with bathrooms and free hot chocolate to help you warm up.

A bit closer to the village is Lake George Recreation center. This too has a great hill, but as its very steep, it's only for snowtubing.

46. Ski or Snowboard

Nearby West Mountain in Queensbury is a favorite of local skiers and snowboarders. There are two main reasons why I would tell visitors to that it's worth their while to go here. First, although it does have intermediate and advanced terrain, it's a fantastic mountain for beginners, young children, and those that are feeling a little rusty. In particular, their bunny hill is perfect for learning or getting your ski legs back. Secondly, it can be very expensive to ski, especially for families.

West Mountain is far more affordable than the larger mountains, and they have great mid-week deals. You'll find these great deals on Monday and Tuesday nights, as well as Friday morning and early afternoon. You'll practically have the mountain to yourself during most weekdays, so you might want to consider skipping very crowded weekend days.

47. Snowshoe Day and Night

Winter truly transforms this area into a white wonderland. Snow can give hiking trails a completely different look and feel than is experienced during the warmer months. Even though there are many places to snowshoe, these are some of my favorites. Gurney Lane just south of the outlets is a great place for beginners and children. If you don't have snowshoes with you, you can borrow some from the park, free of charge. They have a pretty extensive trail system that varies from beginner to advanced. It's a beautiful trek through the woods for all levels of ability. As a plus, you can warm up with complimentary hot chocolate when you are finished.

If you are feeling more adventurous, the Shelving Rock trail on the east side of Lake George is a fun and mildly challenging snowshoe along a series of switchbacks. Once you reach the peak, you'll have the best view you can get all year as it is unobstructed by leaves. Please note, if you go here during the winter, the road to and from the trailhead can be icy and steep. D

Although it is outside of the immediate Lake George area, snowshoeing from Garnet Hill Lodge in North River is definitely worth a mention. If necessary, you can rent snowshoes here for a small fee. The rental shop parking lot butts up to NY state trails, one of which leads to an abandoned garnet mine. It's a short trip, but worth the climb as you'll have great views at the top and be able to stand among the impressive garnet cliffs. You can also lengthen your trip by taking a loop through gorgeous forests and past the pond. You'll eventually come back to the main trail near the parking lot. Once a month in the winter, Garnet Hill lodge does moonlight snowshoe events that are worth looking into.

A few miles south of Lake George Village in Glens Falls, you can snowshoe the Coles Woods trails day or night. The trails are lit at night until 10:30, giving you nice, peaceful woods almost to yourself. It's also great place for getting in some first tracks on snow days.

48. Attend Festivals in Spring and Summer

One thing I truly appreciate about this area is that there is always something to do. The townships are great at providing entertaining festivals and events all year. This is nowhere near a comprehensive list, but just some of the highlights we enjoy as locals.

In the spring, come catch fireworks before the summer crowds arrive. Memorial Day weekend is the unofficial start to summer, and you'll find warm weather and plenty of activities, but with a little more elbow room this time of year.

If you really want a piece of local flavor, try the June LARAC arts festival in Glens Falls. Besides local artists, you'll also find tasty local treats such as fresh maple products, jams, honey, and so much more.

Even though it's not really a festival, Roger's Park has great free events on Tuesday and Wednesday nights in the summer. On Tuesday nights, you can enjoy free concerts (by local and regional artists) set up against the backdrop of marvelous mountains. Wednesday nights offer free, family-friendly movies in the same location. For either occasion, make sure to bring your own chair or blanket (and bug spray).

49. Attend Festivals in the Fall and Winter

The Lake George area is still alive and well, full of activities into the autumn season. You can check local listings for a full list, but I wanted to discuss perhaps the most popular fall event-the September Adirondack Balloon Festival. It is an amazing and impressive sight to see colorful hot-air balloons rise up and dot the sky over the region. However, the problem with popular events is that they are well, popular. That means large crowds and massive amounts of backed-up traffic. We tried to go our first year of living in the area, and we ended up completely missing the whole thing as we were stuck in miles worth of traffic. I'm sure this is the frustration of many who want to attend. Since then, we've learned a thing or two about doing the balloon festival local style.

If you want to be close up to the action, go early in the morning. Weather conditions dictate that the best times to send the hot-air balloons up are during early morning and early evening. Since early morning (5:30-6am) draws less people, you'll have a better chance of getting close to the balloons and being able to chat with balloonists.

You don't need to be right where the balloons go up in order to see them. In fact, I often see balloons going up right from the mall parking lot on Aviation Road. However, a more scenic viewing would be from the top of Prospect Mountain. It's <u>a few</u> miles away from the main action and you will see the balloons only from a distance, but it does give an expansive view of the area as well as being able to see where some of the balloons travel. Best bet is to bring your binoculars!

Life in the area slows down during our cold winters, but Lake George comes back to life in February for the month-long winter festival (weekends only). There are plenty of events, but I find that unless you're a participant in many of these, they hold little interest for most. However, during this time, the lake is usually frozen to its deepest (some winters in recent years have been too mild for deep freeze). Ice can be so thick that I've seen helicopters land on the frozen lake during this time. Many take advantage of the thick ice to walk out into the middle of the lake. It might seem scary at first (make sure you check ice depths and obey any posted warnings), but if you brave it, you'll have a unique view of the lake that you won't get any other time of year.

The winter festival continues at night with fireworks each Saturday after dark. A huge bonfire is built on the beach in Shepard's Park so you can grab a hot drink and warm yourself around the fire as you watch the fireworks. Definitely a great end to a winter's day.

50. If You Only Have One Day

This is really a tough one. There are so many great things to see and do, how do I narrow it down? I'm going to give it my best shot.

- If you want to see the lake, take a daytime boat tour. Some are short and you will have an up-close view of the scenery.
- If you want a great eating experience, the Sagamore Hotel has a number of restaurants with good food and great lake views.
- If you want to take a quick peek at some leaves (or just the whole area), head to the top of Prospect Mountain and make sure to stop off at the other lookouts on the way up.
- Grab some local wine, honey, or maple syrup
- Go to the beach in Bolton Landing
- Watch the fireworks

The very best advice I can give you? Try to stay longer!

Janie Hirschklau

Top Reasons to Book This Trip

- Stunning mountain scenery and crystal-clear waters
- There is always something for everyone
- It's an outdoor paradise. If you don't want to spend your day indoors, this is the place to be.

Janie Hirschklau

> TOURIST

GREATER THAN A TOURIST

Visit GreaterThanATourist.com
http://GreaterThanATourist.com

Sign up for the Greater Than a Tourist
Newsletter
http://eepurl.com/cxspyf

Follow us on Facebook:
https://www.facebook.com/GreaterThanATourist

Follow us on Pinterest:
http://pinterest.com/GreaterThanATourist

Follow us on Instagram:
http://Instagram.com/GreaterThanATourist

Janie Hirschklau

> TOURIST

GREATER THAN A TOURIST

Please leave your honest review of this book on Amazon and Goodreads. Thank you.

We appreciate your positive and negative feedback as we try to provide tourist guidance in their next trip from a local.

> TOURIST

GREATER THAN A TOURIST

You can find Greater Than a Tourist books on Amazon.

Janie Hirschklau

> TOURIST

GREATER THAN A TOURIST

WHERE WILL YOU TRAVEL TO NEXT?

Janie Hirschklau

> TOURIST

GREATER THAN A TOURIST

Our Story

Traveling is a passion of this series creator. She studied abroad in college, and for their honeymoon Lisa and her husband toured Europe. During her travels to Malta, an older man tried to give her some advice based on his own experience living on the island since he was a young boy. She thought he was just trying to sell her something. When traveling to some places she was wary to talk to locals because she was afraid that they weren't being genuine. She created this book series to give you as a tourist an inside view on the place you are exploring and the ability to learn what locals would like to tell tourist. A topic that they are very passionate about.

Janie Hirschklau

> TOURIST

GREATER THAN A TOURIST

Notes

Made in United States
North Haven, CT
01 August 2022

22090420R00064